Home Place

poems by

Linda Caldwell

Finishing Line Press
Georgetown, Kentucky

Home Place

Copyright © 2016 by Linda Caldwell
ISBN 978-1-944899-77-6 First Edition
All rights reserved under International and Pan-American Copyright Conventions.
No part of this book may be reproduced in any manner whatsoever without written permission from the publisher, except in the case of brief quotations embodied in critical articles and reviews.

ACKNOWLEDGMENTS

Poems included in *Home Place* appeared in some form in the following journals or anthologies. I thank the editors for having faith in me.

Appalachian Connections: "Generations of Farmers"
Appalachian Heritage: "Angel of Death"
Astropoetica: Mapping Stars through Poetry: "Looking for Summer's Door"
Carnegie I: "A Gardener's Watch"
Chaffin Journal: "Farm Woman," "Skin and Bone Box," "Predator and Prey"
Kentucky Authors Cook: " In My Mother's Kitchen"
Kaleidowhirl: A Literary Journal: "Leap Year"
Of Woods and Waters: A Kentucky Outdoor Reader: "Predator and Prey"
RiverSedge: "In the Churchyard"

Publisher: Leah Maines

Editor: Christen Kincaid

Cover Art: Loretta Adams

Author Photo: Mary Owens

Cover Design: Elizabeth Maines

Printed in the USA on acid-free paper.
Order online: www.finishinglinepress.com
also available on amazon.com

Author inquiries and mail orders:
Finishing Line Press
P. O. Box 1626
Georgetown, Kentucky 40324
U. S. A.

Table of Contents

In the Churchyard 1
Artifacts 2
After the First Cut 3
November Trees 4
Autumn Blues 5
Generations of Farmers 7
Rituals 9
In My Mother's Kitchen 10
Angel of Death 11
Resurrection Ground 12
Near A Bridge in a Secluded Wood 13
Roundhill 14
Gone Things 15
Flagwoman on a Dangerous Curve 16
Horses and Moons 17
Queen of Cowgirls 18
Imprinted 19
Two Deer Rhetorical 20
Skin and Bone Box 21
Predator and Prey 22
Leap Year 23
Looking for Summer's Door 24

In memory of
Edna Petrey Caldwell
George Thomas Caldwell
James Forga Caldwell

In the Churchyard

The car shivers with wind's assault.
I feel earth's revolution.

Under leafless trees, grass waves
like Kansas wheat mimicking oceans.

December, warm enough to put the top down—
I spin in brightness.

I cling, tilt, turn, wait,
grow no wiser through the passing seasons.

Still, I write poems.

Artifacts

While clouds gather against the mountains,
March, unleashed, howls around the eaves.

Objects blow and wash: a pocket from a rotted jacket flaps
beside the garden gate; from the underworld a forgotten red eye blinks.

Flecks of window glass and flow-blue china dot my path.
Arrowheads prick fresh-smelling, plowed bottomlands.

Only Leo, far above, watches
as I stalk treasures no one knows
but me and those who left them behind.

After the First Cut

When tobacco wagons rattle
planks and slow down on the curve,
they draw both my ear and eye.

Brown men plant
their feet on poplar rails.
Spanish and English mix orders
and conversation, echoes
to my father's lost words.

Dying plants droop westward
in opposition to your face turned
toward resurrection morning.

The footprint of your barn remains
where once you handed-off sticks,
heavy with plants
that threw shadow over me.

The past swallows tomorrow.

You have been gone
longer than I had you.

November Trees

I call the names of the dead,
hackberry, persimmon, sycamore,
an ancient locust tree named
bird tree where a screech owl made its nest,
another named cat tree
for a reason no one alive remembers.

Cedar twins survive broken-limbed by a tornado.
They witnessed my father's birth,
in this house underneath their thin shadows.
Was it a day like today
bereft of sunlight?
Or a day with sunlight balancing
on spiny, cedar needles?

His other trees are ghosts
of memory, too, even the tulip poplar
he planted in the last year of his life.

Trees grow faster
and die sooner
since his death.

Autumn Blues

1
Your desertion shot
through me
when I opened
the red Liberty gate,
my fingers placed
where yours marked
the cold dew on steel.

I track your ghost
calling cattle, a sound
between moan and wail
that I would recognize
standing on the moon
instead of this sun-scorched grass.

My desires trundle, one after the other
like steers lured by the scent of salt.

Should I turn back or follow, panting
like my neutered hounds?

2
I walk a crazed path
among patterns of ironweed.
The bucket and box
where you fed the sick calf
rot on the ground.

The cattle are sold.
Your spoor is cold.
I wanted to go with you
with all of my blood and sinew,
teeth and nails.

A gnawing remains
like dogs burrowing
into a voles nest.

I cry, "Come back,"
but only echoes answer.

Generations of Farmers

1
Within the dormant, winter woods
a patch of white traps the eyes.
Nestled in the crotch of a fallen tree,
a newborn lies like drifted snow.
Perhaps his mother hid him out
as cows often do.

Cloud shadows float
over pure Charolais.
Did his ears flap,
or did the wind lift
and drop them?

Whisper a name.
One deep eye opens.
I won't count his bones
among my broken lost
midst limestone scatter.

Tell the young farmer his new calf rests
near the landmark, spalted oak.

2
The ghost of my father stirs.

A film of memory—
on the coldest day of the year,
a dry Guernsey does not follow
the milkers in at dusk.

The older herdsman searches
the naked woods and sinkholes
where cows tend to hide
when giving birth until he finds her
and her newborn in a pawpaw thicket.

He shoulders the calf to our hearth.
If the mother won't nurse,
he and my mother will feed him
formula from a bottle, keep him near
until his gawky legs lift him.

Rituals

Within a bare-bulbed circle of light,
he skins the dead calf
and places its hide over the orphan.

Under the smell of blood, milk, and last year's tobacco,
his wife halters the splay-legged mother.

Squirting milk on the baby's head, he anoints.
The woman hums.

They hope the cow will smell her own scent,
her baby's skin, and allow nursing.

But after dodging heels and head, they give up,
feed the orphan from bottle and bucket.

Months later a Charolais bull, like a puppy,
follows them along the fence row.

The wife's perfect toes bruised sacrifice
to patience and rough affection.

In My Mother's Kitchen

I thought painting over her tulip-yellow walls
with a skimmed-milk blue would banish her.
She despised blue.
But I forgot the old kitchen,
where I now sleep,
was bead and batten, covered
with grandmother's buttermilk blue.
Mother didn't flee the hated hue.
She made a new kitchen
that under her hands moved
from 40s to 70s like lard to canola.

I gave up the struggle to exile her,
kept her metal-based sink,
second-hand formica table,
rustic cabinets that my uncle built,
and her teapots.

In other rooms, ghosts departed
when I moved their chairs.
But my mother comes into the kitchen
pulls up a stool and asks for a cup of tea with milk.

Angel of Death

The coyote glides golden
across the eastern slope
of Levi Wilder's farm, where once
my mother saw white mules fly over
the wooden gate and dirt road
like the angel of death
departing the parlor
where John Guinn lay a corpse.

Resurrection Ground
    Boatwright Family Graveyard

tree spirits shake leaves
stones lean under full moon
cows breathe in dark

tumbled stones by cow and tree
two hundred years of rain
from springs and wells
we drink their bones

Near a Bridge in a Secluded Wood

Blue light pastes thin limbs
against the sky.
Haze floats among bare, narrow trunks.
A darker grey shadows the center
of weathered wood, beckoning.

From water born
before the arch spanned
the hidden stream,
mist rises
through air breathed
by the first people.

The one who crosses over
disappears inside sparseness,
leaves behind visible breath.

Hoarding the last green,
hardy bee asters refuse surrender,
murmur in wind with the water below—

"Too soon, too soon."

Roundhill

These ghosts will not sleep forever.
Dragging Canoe's prophecy
for a dark and bloody ground
echoes around me as the fingers
of Tecumseh and Black Fish trail
my spine. We live on resurrection ground.

Gone Things

Every spring, as soon as the weather breaks,
she hunts the remaining prickly pear cactus
on the hill that erodes down
to the spring-fed branch of water.
Each year she fears its colony will be gone
like the shag-bark hickories
that once shaded peanut-butter picnics.
Perhaps every gone thing is claimed
and shrunken by spirit folk who live
in underground hollows formed
by the persistence of water on limestone.

Flagwoman on a Dangerous Curve

The dog tilts his head over clumps of tough grass,
listens for voles tunneling underground.

After buffering leaves fall
and song birds and insects depart,
the interstate's rumble
a couple of ridges over
seems closer.

Glimmerings hover ready
to dart as the vole might
from the hummock the dog attends.

Turning my ear toward the unseen,
I am a flagwoman caught
between the world of cars and animals
and the world where
gone things whisper.

I balance on the verge,
a flag of merging lanes of time.

Horses and Moons

I remember a long-legged girl
and wide-backed workhorses with manes
like scrub brushes
from poll to that vulnerable hollow
between the withers.

She rides Molly bareback
and Beck plods along beside.
Harnesses jingle as they descend
to barn lot and house after tobacco setting—
a long day for horses and men.

The girl's mind is empty of everything
except horse scent, warm sun, and the green of May—
years to come are as far away as the pale sky

with the daylight moon,
a sickle to slice between girl and woman.

Queen of Cowgirls

Lowing brings me up from bed
to light a candle.

pity the lost calves

Muzzy-headed I watch
the herd in creamy light
as they crunch through morning ice.

pity cold cows

Before I sleep
they follow me with their eyes
and speak to me
under whiskery breaths.

pity doomed steers

They huddle under the hill.

If they were mine, I would lift
their stolidness in my arms
and carry it over the threshold.

Imprinted
>*for Patty Wren Smith*

Wren said, "When observing
the natural world, look for shapes,
sharpen your vision, key your eyes
to the caterpillar, and to the pattern
of its droppings below the eaten leaf."

The opposite of my mother's advice *don't look for snakes,
and you won't see snakes.*

But for me every small thing morphs
into bird: in autumn's last mulberry leaf
is a wren, in spring, a muddy spot
on the road, a dove, and in winter,
a red-tailed hawk's silhouette looms
over a rock pile.

In summer, birds appear everywhere
as sound, spirit, form.
The hibiscus is a cardinal, a day lily an oriole,
wildflowers, a choir of buntings and finches.

Two Deer Rhetorical

Are these the deer
I saw a year ago,
who were so curious
that they came close,
then moved away,
coming near again
and again.
Are they messengers,
angels, my ghosts,
or only skin, muscle,
hair and bone?
Whatever they are
they do not fear me
nor do I them, this time—
with the fence between.

Skin and Bone Box
> *What is body if not memories and stories?*
> Yogi Amanda Smith

Anvil, stirrup and drum cadence
telling-story voices of the old ones.

With tingles and tics scars remind me
of bicycle wrecks and surgeries.

Books continue to carve dents in my arms.

Ultrasound reveals the moonscape
of my right breast.

And receptors in the nose shoot
memory straight to the brain—

coal smoke: Lancaster, England
and tobacco stripping rooms.

On the tongue, tea tastes of
my child's wild bergamot garden
where bee-mimic moths
etched my retina in infrared.

My legs remember
I walked before I crawled.

Predator and Prey

On the farm across the creek
a drama plays in the morning mist.
Dogs bay.
My dogs answer
with territorial barks.

I see a white-tailed deer taking fences
like the athlete it is.

I find my binoculars.
The deer's long gone.
A mutt and Walker hound
nose the ground, tails moving to and fro.

My neighbor, a farmer, watches, too.
From his rigid stance
I know his agenda differs from mine.
maybe he condemns
the hunting dogs as nuisances
or considers the running deer
a destroyer of crops.

I want to hunt with only my eyes,
pull every pleasure with my senses.

Before I return to duties,
I lecture my dogs about their safe, charmed lives.
They tilt their heads and try to understand.

I never know the ending of this morning's drama,
but I think everyone turns out with their own treasure
except perhaps the farmer.

Leap Year

Through a blue window,
deer walk the horizon like my ghosts.
The creek reflects a creamy sky.

Turning from olive to yellow,
finches flock the mulberry tree.

Spring month begins tomorrow,
but as the old ones say,
I haven't made it to grass.
In the new light,
the frost-killed,
fescue-covered,
gray hills seem
bright white.

Smoke drifts above
my neighbor's chimney.
His thorn trees prick
at my morning.

I strain to catch a lost dream,
reach for the kettle,
forgetting it scorched,
and was discarded months ago.

Looking for Summer's Door

The Teapot of Sagittarius
pours above the gentle line
of southern mountains.

The Lagoon Nebula hovers
above its spout like steam.
All spring I waited
for its first sighting.
When I finally find the city of light,
I know I am across summer's threshold.

As the teapot slides
toward the equinox,
I grieve.

When Orion begins his wide stride across
approaching hungry nights,
the warm cover
of spring and summer float away.
Remembered winters find my bones.
Like a cat, I hunt the door to summer.

Linda Caldwell has lived most of her life along a two mile stretch of Paint Lick Creek where the Bluegrass meets Appalachia.

In addition to being a school librarian for twenty-seven years in Jefferson County Public Schools, she also has been a volunteer and board member for Friends of Paint Lick, Incorporated, an award winning, grassroots community service organization.

Her poetry has been published in journals and anthologies, including *Coe Review, Pearl, Prairie Schooner, Tears in the Fence (UK), Motif: Writing by Ear, Newgrowth, Writing Who We Are, Of Woods and Waters: A Kentucky Outdoors Reader,* and *This Wretched Vessel.*

As a playwright, she has had plays staged at Berea College Theatre Laboratory, Berea Arena Theater, and at the Artists Collaborative Theatre in Elkhorn City, Kentucky. She is the recipient of two Kentucky Foundation for Women grants to work with residents in an assisted living facility in Richmond.

www.ingramcontent.com/pod-product-compliance
Lightning Source LLC
LaVergne TN
LVHW050046090426
835510LV00043B/3332